What Shall We Do With This Baby?

A Christmas Eve
Worship Service

Jan Spence

CSS Publishing Company, Inc.
Lima, Ohio

WHAT SHALL WE DO WITH THIS BABY?

Scripture quotations are from the *New Revised Standard Version of the Bible*, copyright 1989 by the Division of Christian Education of the National Council of the Churches of Christ in the USA. Used by permission.

9355 / ISBN 1-55673-655-X

Dedicated to my six children:
Kirk, Laurie, Cam,
Kerry, Jeremy and Jason

Table Of Contents

Introduction

A simple retelling of the Christmas Story in scripture and song was the request of my pastor for our Sunday school Christmas program. I agreed, but as I sat in choir looking out at our less than 100-member country church, two things concerned me.

First, how could we, one more time, "do" the Mary, Joseph and baby story in a way that would in the tiniest degree capture the wonder, joy and significance of that event? Our Sunday school youth were an active, creative, hands-on, get-involved-in group of kids. They were small in number but big in ideas. What was the Christmas story for them?

Second, seemingly important, but still perplexing to me was how was I to choose a baby Jesus from among the four new babies in our church family?

I sat watching them. They were all there, and I thought about them — Hanna, held by her dad, and then passed down the pew, hugged, kissed and played with in turn by her brother and sister, to arrive smiling into the arms of her mother. Lucky baby, to be so loved!

Several seats back was Kyle, also in the arms of a loving family. He had been so sober and quiet when he arrived. All that curly blond hair that was so dull now shown like new gold. What had his life been like before this family took him in? The unanswerable question was how could they bear to give him up — especially the girls who knew all too well what it meant to be "foster kids"? What a celebration the day they were adopted. Would it happen for Kyle?

Adopted, the word had no meaning for Megan just now. Fair, tiny, so fragile looking, her parents waited six years for her and they were there to bring her home from the hospital the day after she was born. She will have no difficulty believing adoption is spelled love.

And Katlin, our entire congregation waited and prayed for her safe arrival. We got the reports from Guatemala, via a bad telephone connection. "You've been accepted as adoptive parents. A baby will be born soon. It's a girl. She's being screened. She's healthy. Papers have been signed. Papers are delayed." And finally, "She's cleared to leave Guatemala." The news was shared with us Sunday by Sunday as the anxious parents-to-be waited and worried. Who will ever forget the outpouring of love and joy for this new little family on their first Sunday in church.

Then my eyes fell on my son. At 16 he was six-feet tall, poised and competent in his task, a far cry from that frightened, crying, bruised and angry two-year-old the social worker brought to our door. In the back pew was his brother, seated with his dad. I saw my husband lean over and whisper something to him and I guessed plans for a fun afternoon were in the making. We have four natural children and we certainly didn't plan on adopting two little brothers, but when we found out the boys were to be kept in separate foster homes and be long-term wards of the state, it seemed the most natural thing in the world to adopt them.

I didn't hear much of the sermon that morning. Instead, a Christmas pageant was forming in my mind. We would use all the babies scene by scene. The brothers and sisters and all the children and youth would explore the roles of Mary and Joseph in the baby's life. We would discover the roles of the shepherds, wise men and angels and their ways of caring for a helpless baby.

The story of every baby's birth is the Christmas story. It is that story over and over again. Only the people involved determine the story's outcome. The question became: what shall we do with this baby?

From this, our entire program Advent/Christmas became "Babies, Christmas 1991." It culminated with our Christmas Eve service.

Jan Spence
December 1991

Final Note

Our congregation is small but unique. This year we had four babies added to our numbers. One baby was born to natural parents. One baby was adopted from Guatemala and another was adopted from an area agency. The fourth baby is a foster baby.

Each of the scenes used one of the babies. In scenes 2, 3 and 4 Mary and Joseph were also different children. The Sunday school department collected baby items for a local teen pregnancy center. The children's Christmas tree was decorated with baby rattles and things a baby needs. The emphasis was what Christ did for us and how we are called to help others, especially the helpless infant.

Babies

The children of our congregation became involved in our theme. Many of the following ideas were their own. Others came from Sunday school teachers and parents.

A Baby Tree — The children have their own small, live tree in our fellowship hall. They chose to decorate it with new and used baby rattles. A baby blanket served as a tree skirt and good, used stuffed animals were donated and placed underneath.

Baby Shopping — The children earned and saved money for a shopping trip. Arrangements were made to take our youth to a local second-hand store. There children were selective and purchased many items of clothing, blankets and sleepers.

Gift-wrapping Party — The children wrapped their gifts in donated baby paper and made paper chains of the scraps to add to their tree.

We invited a member of our congregation to talk with our youth about "Phoenix House," a local group home for unwed mothers and their babies. This talk concentrated on the needs of babies. After this session, our youth decided to send their gifts to this house. At a later date we arranged a tour of the home for our youth.

Our entire congregation was invited to become involved in our "babies" project. On the evening of our program, many adults, not previously involved in our project, brought baby gifts to place under the tree.

Program Notes

Announced by youth or pastor — Familiar Christmas hymns were chosen for singing by the congregation. These may be announced or the lights may be turned on for singing.

Sound system operated by youth — Questioner 1 and 2 are stationed with hand microphones at the front left and right in sanctuary. Storyteller with microphone speaks from back right. Scripture narrator with microphone reads from back left.

Lights operated by youth — Spotlight focuses on "baby alone" and highlights manger setting (three).

Teachers behind the scenes — Children are costumed as groups and are supervised by a Sunday school teacher. Children enter by groups from the side or back of the sanctuary. When each scene concludes, children may sit in front of the church or return to their parents' pews.

Cast includes: angels, shepherds, wise men, Joseph (3), Mary (3), babies (4)

All children sing — "Away In A Manger," and "Go Tell It On The Mountain."

Youth provide invitation to audience to bring gifts to the fellowship hall and place them under the baby tree and enjoy refreshments and fellowship following the service.

All children from ages 2 through sixth grade may participate in costume. All youth from grades seven through twelve may participate in announcing, reading, lighting and sound.

Babies (4) were held by Sunday school teachers and then placed into the arms of Mary and Joseph (older children, brothers and sisters) when possible. Infants were returned to parents at the end of each scene.

Order Of Worship

Piano prelude *(Fades to a dark chancel. Spotlight picks up a baby alone in a cardboard box or manger.)*

What Shall We Do With This Baby?
> Scene 1
> Scene 2
> Scene 3
> Scene 4

Prayer:
Dear Heavenly Parent:
New life is so precious and so fragile. You entrusted your son and your plan of salvation to human hands and hearts. May we be aware as never before of our human responsibility for your heavenly plan. Please grant us the will to love anew every child born on this earth. May the old familiar story of the birth of your son renew the hope that each child can live according to your plan. In the name of the infant Jesus who lived and died to become the Savior of the world. Amen.

Meditation *(from pastor or program director)*

Other options follow
Individuals and families in our church have already responded in their own way. We have invited several of them to share their story with us.
- Foster parents
- Adoptive parents
- Step parents
- Single parents

Encourage children to share their experiences and feelings.
- Foster children
- Adopted
- Step
- Single

(Note: These are extremely sensitive areas and much thought and care and support must be available to those who are willing to share. Each situation will be different.)

Thank you *(from Sunday school department or pastor)*

Invitation to "giving of gifts" and fellowship *(youth)*

(Follow children to the baby tree)

13

What Shall We Do With This Baby?

Scene 1

Spotlight on a lone baby in a manger
Two readers/questioners and a narrator

Q1: What is that?

Q2: A baby!

Q1: A baby! Alone?

Q2: Alone! Where did it come from?

Q1: How did it get here?

Q2: Whose is it?

Q1: Where are its parents?

Q2: Is it hungry?

Q1: Is it sick?

Q2: Is it afraid?

Q1: Who will protect it?

Q2: Was anyone glad it was born?

Q1: Did the neighbors know about it?

Q2: Does it have any brothers and sisters?

Q1: What of its future?

Q2: How can this be? A baby alone . . . .

Q1: Is there no one in the whole world to love and care for this child?

Narrator: What shall we do with this baby? This is the question that has echoed through time. Nothing is more helpless and needy than an infant alone. Without human help a baby alone cannot thrive or survive. What shall we do with this baby indeed!

Scene 2

An empty manger
Two readers/questioners, a narrator and a scripture reader

Congregation sings: "What Child Is This?" as Mary and Joseph enter carrying a baby.

Scripture reader: Luke 2:1-7
In those days a decree went out from Emperor Augustus that all the world should be registered. This was the first registration and was taken while Quirinius was governor of Syria. All went to their own towns to be registered. Joseph also went from the town of Nazareth in Galilee to Judea, to the city of David called Bethlehem, because he was descended from the house and family of David. He went to be registered with Mary, to whom he was engaged and who was expecting a child. While they were there, the time came for her to deliver her child. And she gave birth to her firstborn son and wrapped him in bands of cloth, and laid him in a manger, because there was no place for them in the inn.

Congregation sings: "Silent Night" (verse 1, 3)

Narrator: What a beautiful story. Best of all it is more than a story. It really happened on that night long ago and it shows us the way God planned it to be for his Son. The loving arms and boundless love of a gentle mother. Beside her the wise, strong, protecting father. All the needs of this helpless baby would be lovingly met.

Q1: Yes, but what of the countless children who are born and one or both of the birth parents do not fit these images?

Q2: Are they doomed to be members of the 5-H club? The hungry, the homeless, the healthless, the hugless and the hopeless? Or does God have another plan for these?

16

Narrator: Of course God does. They are called foster mothers, foster fathers, step-mothers, step-fathers, adoptive mothers, adoptive fathers, or maybe aunt or uncle, grandma or grandpa, brother or sister. The title does not matter. They have the true heart of a mother or father and the ability to care for, protect and love any child placed in their care.

Q1: I am beginning to feel better about this. But is a loving parent, or even two parents, all a baby needs in this world?

Scene 3

Mary, Joseph and baby in the manger
Two readers/questioners, narrator, scripture reader, angels and
shepherds

Congregation sings: "Joy To The World"
(Angels enter and gather around the manger.)

Scripture reader: Luke 2:8-16
   In that region there were shepherds living in the fields keeping watch over their flock by night. Then an angel of the Lord stood before them, and the glory of the Lord shone around them, and they were terrified. But the angel said to them, "Do not be afraid; for see — I am bringing you good news of great joy for all the people: to you is born this day in the city of David a Savior, who is the Messiah, the Lord. This will be a sign for you: you will find a child wrapped in bands of cloth and lying in a manger." And suddenly there was with the angel a multitude of the heavenly host, praising God and saying: "Glory to God in the highest heaven and on earth peace among those whom he favors."
   When the angels had left them and gone into heaven, the shepherds said to one another, "Let us go now to Bethlehem and see this thing that has taken place, which the Lord has made known to us." So they went with haste and found Mary and Joseph, and the child lying in the manger.

Congregation sings: "While Shepherds Watched Their Flocks"
(Angels move back and shepherds gather around the manger.)

Children sing: "Away In A Manger"

Narrator: What joy! What rejoicing and what wonder! And rightly so, for this baby is God's own Son, born to be the Savior of the world. Good news indeed! No wonder the shepherds returned glorifying and praising God!

Children sing: "Go Tell It On The Mountain"
(Angels and shepherds return to their seats)

Q1: Angels announced Jesus' birth. Wow! The last birth announcement I saw had a blue teddy bear on it and was sent with a 29 cent postage stamp.

Q2: Yes, but the joy was there and the person receiving it rejoiced. Isn't that what counts?

Q1: You are right. I still can't help but think of the baby who is born and no one celebrates its birth. It must make God sad, too.

Narrator: I'm sure it does. That is one reason to celebrate Jesus' birth. It reminds us that in our hearts, we are the parents, angels and shepherds. We must rejoice at the birth of every child because of the possibilities we see in him or her. It is called hope!

Scene 4

Mary, Joseph and baby
Two readers/questioners, narrator, scripture reader, and wise
men

Narrator: Hope, what a beautiful word. Hope in the form of a baby. It is God's way of proclaiming that the world should go on, and just think, it puts the responsibility right on us.

Q1: I was getting to that. Yes, a baby needs love, caring, joy at his or her birth, people to be supportive, but then what? God's Son was born in a stable, with a manger for a bed. His parents were poor. They were in a strange town. How were they going to provide for this baby's future needs?

Q2: Is there any more to the story?

Congregation sings: "We Three Kings" (verse 1)
(Wise men enter with gifts)

Scripture reader: Matthew 2:1-2, 9-12
In the time of King Herod, after Jesus was born in Bethlehem of Judea, wise men from the East came to Jerusalem, asking, "Where is the child who has been born king of the Jews? For we observed his star at its rising, and have come to pay him homage."
When they had heard the king, they set out; and there, ahead of them, went the star that they had seen at its rising, until it stopped over the place where the child was. When they saw that the star had stopped, they were overwhelmed with joy. On entering the house, they saw the child with Mary his mother; and they knelt down and paid him homage. Then, opening their treasure chests, they offered him gifts of gold, frankincense and myrrh. And having been warned in a dream not to return to Herod, they left for their own country by another road.

Narrator: The wise men did come to worship, but they did not come empty handed. The gifts they brought were surely an investment for the future needs of a growing child. It seems right that human hearts and human hands were needed to provide for God's Son. Just look ahead to what he was going to provide for us!

Q1: It is coming very clear now. It is very simple really. Jesus came as a helpless baby, as God's Son, to bring us salvation.

Q2: And as parents, angels, shepherds and wise men we must do everything we can possibly do to save every child! With our love, our joy, our rejoicing and our gifts!

Narrator: So the question will echo on. What shall we do with this baby? And each of us will answer it in our own way.

www.ingramcontent.com/pod-product-compliance
Lightning Source LLC
Chambersburg PA
CBHW071813020426
42331CB00008B/2483